PEN AND PRINTING PRESS

Pen and

Printing Press

The Story of the National Lutheran Editors' and Managers' Association and Its Work

1913-1957

Material compiled from Minutes
By JAMES A. RYBERG

AUGUSTANA PRESS
ROCK ISLAND, ILLINOIS

PEN AND PRINTING PRESS

Copyright, 1957, by
NATIONAL LUTHERAN EDITORS' AND
MANAGERS' ASSOCIATION

⟦PRINTED IN U·S·A·⟧

AUGUSTANA BOOK CONCERN
Printers and Binders
Rock Island, Illinois
1957

Foreword

WHEN JOHANNES GUTENBERG in 1452 invented moveable type for printing, he little realized how potent an instrument he had placed in the hands of his fellow men. But things do not happen by blind chance. To the thinking soul, God's hand may always be clearly discerned in human history. Scarcely six decades had passed after Gutenberg's epoch-making discovery before the blows of Luther's hammer on Wittenberg's chapel door were heard reverberating around the world, and, thanks to the art of printing, the Ninety-five Theses were soon being read avidly in every corner of Europe.

For Luther and his contemporaries were not slow in making use of this powerful weapon which God in His providence had placed in their hands, and it can hardly be denied that it was the printing press, more than any other human instrumentality, that gave wings to the truths of the Reformation.

In the planting of the Lutheran Church in America, the followers of Martin Luther have not forgotten this lesson from the Reformation. As early as 1696 there was printed in Stockholm, Sweden, the celebrated translation of Luther's Catechism into the language of the Algonquian Indians. This was the work of the Rev. Johannes Campanius, a zealous and devout pastor and missionary who had labored in the Delaware Colony from 1642 to 1648, and was undoubtedly the first piece of Lutheran literature printed for the exclusive purpose of propagating the faith in America.

In the centuries that followed, as the migration of Lutherans from the lands of northern Europe to America reached flood tide, it was the printing press that continually came to the aid of heroic pastor-missionaries who were seeking to bring the Word of Life to their countrymen in the New World. The whole story of our church press in America has been very largely the story of spiritual leaders with faith and vision who saw very clearly that the spoken word must be supplemented by the written word. In a sense, the church paper and other devotional literature became the first home missionaries of our Church. They possessed the advantage of being able to reach many isolated places where the messenger of the Gospel was unable to go, and they entered tens of thousands of homes where the voice of the preacher was seldom or never heard.

They also reminded the confessing Christians of their responsibility as witnesses for Christ in the task of planting the Church. They called on believers to establish schools where men might be prepared for the Gospel ministry; to reveal compassion toward the sick, the poor, the friendless, the orphan and the widow; to remember peoples walking in darkness, and to send forth messengers of the Gospel to the far corners of the earth. Thus, they contributed mightily in laying the foundations of our Lutheran Zion in the New World and in promoting its spiritual enterprises.

It would indeed be a most fascinating story could we reveal how our various Lutheran bodies in this country adopted the printing press as one of their chief allies, and how they began to establish publication houses and to edit church papers. But that is not the object of this volume. Rather, its purpose is to tell how those charged with the responsibility for our Lutheran publications came together nearly half a century ago to form what has claimed to be the oldest inter-synodical group in America, namely, the National Lutheran Editors' and Managers' Association. Nor is it intended that this shall be a chronological history of the Association. Instead, its purpose is to give an insight into the thinking of the organization, the problems with which it has grappled, and the leadership it has given to our Lutheran household of faith. For, let it be said in all humility, the Lutheran editors and managers have not been content with merely recording contemporary history, they have insisted on helping to make it. In this prophetic role, they have often been instrumental in blazing a trail in many areas of the Church's life, not least of all in the strivings for Lutheran unity.

In order to make available to the student of church history a record of the significant events and pronouncements in the life of the Association, an editorial committee consisting of Dr. O. G. Malmin, editor of the *Lutheran Herald;* Mr. Birger Swenson, general manager of Augustana Book Concern; Mr. Albert Anderson, sales manager of the Augsburg Publishing House, and the undersigned, editor of the *Lutheran Companion,* was appointed to sift the material in the official Minutes of the organization and to put it into printed form. The actual work of collecting and organizing the material was delegated to Mr. James A. Ryberg, assistant director of public relations of the Evangelical Lutheran Church. The results of the committee's labors are submitted in this volume.

E. E. RYDEN

Contents

CHAPTER ONE

Genesis of the Association

THIRTEEN MEN ASSEMBLED around a table in Chicago Lutheran Theological Seminary in Maywood, Ill., on May 22, 1913, to form what is perhaps the oldest pan-Lutheran organization in America—The National Lutheran Editors' Association, now in its 45th year.

Recognizing a need for co-operation and concerted action in dealing with common problems as editors of official Lutheran church periodicals, the members agreed to meet annually and to work toward more complete unity among all Lutherans.

Charter members of the NLEA were:

The Rev. Dr. L. G. Abrahamson, editor of *Augustana,* Rock Island, Ill.;

Mr. A. H. Dornbirer, manager of the Lutheran Book Concern, Columbus, O.;

The Rev. Dr. W. H. Dunbar, pastor, Baltimore, Md.;

The Rev. Dr. F. G. Gotwald, editor of *Lutheran Church Work,* York, Pa.;

The Rev. Dr. W. H. Greever, editor of *American Lutheran Survey,* Columbia, S. C.;

1

Prof. Theodore Graebner, editor of *Lutheraner*, Chicago, Ill.;

Mr. Paulus List, manager of Wartburg Publishing House, Chicago, Ill.;

Mr. Charles B. Opp, manager of General Council Publishing House, Philadelphia, Pa.;

The Rev. Dr. Fr. Richter, editor of *Kirchenblatt*, Clinton, Ia.;

The Rev. Dr. George W. Sandt, editor of *The Lutheran*, Philadelphia, Pa.;

The Rev. Dr. W. E. Schuette, editor of *Lutheran Standard*, Toledo, O.;

The Rev. Dr. C. J. Sodergren, editor of *The Lutheran Companion*, Rock Island, Ill.;

The Rev. Dr. C. A. Wendell, pastor, Evanston, Ill.

* * *

As specified in the constitution, the founders intended membership in the NLEA only for editors of official Lutheran church periodicals and publication managers of such papers. This was amended in 1943 to include "all editors-in-chief and full-time editors of official Lutheran church papers, and all general managers, assistant managers, and circulation managers of Lutheran publication houses."

Five years later, in 1948, the NLEA further amended membership requirements to add: "Editors of other Lutheran papers," election to membership being contingent on written endorsement of editors of two official papers. Such members, however, were not eligible to hold office in the organization.

At its Philadelphia convention in 1955, the NLEA opened its membership to "all editors and full-time assistants of official Lutheran periodicals, journalists serving the Lutheran Church full-time, and editors of other church-connected Lutheran periodicals of national circulation." At the same time, all members became eligible to hold office in the association.

Due to some confusion arising from the interpretation of the above decision, the Editors' Section in 1956, afer conferring with the Managers' Section, named a special committee to draw up a list of all editors and other Lutheran journalists eligible for membership and to submit the list before the 1957 meeting.

* * *

During the NLEA's early years, editors and managers met simultaneously. However, as the membership grew, meetings were held in two separate sections—as a means of facilitating discussion of more specific problems confronting editors and managers, respectively.

Out of these meetings, conducted annually without interruption since 1913, have come the genesis of thought and planning which have not only enriched the various Lutheran bodies represented, but which also have served to draw Lutherans closer together for a more effective impact on American society.

CHAPTER TWO

Contribution to Lutheran Unity

PERHAPS THE GREATEST contribution of the National Lutheran Editors' Association to American Lutheranism has been the group's consistent spurring of the cause for Lutheran unity. As early as 1914, at the infant organization's second meeting, the editors agreed on the desirability of bringing together the various Lutheran bodies in America.

Viewing the situation as it existed at that early date, the editors listed factors standing in the way of Lutheran unity: "Individualism, provincialism, linguistic and national differences, groundless suspicion, and a tendency to be particularistic."

They further noted "disagreement as to the basis on which the Lutheran synodical bodies can come together; and a disposition, when overtures are made, to question the good faith of the body making them."

The objectivity of these observations, formulated 42 years ago, may still be applied to some extent to the picture of Lutheran bodies in existence today. Some of the barriers seen by the 1914 editors have not yet been lowered enough to permit the full Lutheran unity the organization sought then, and which NLEA member editors continue to champion through editorials and special articles even today.

Studying the problem further, the editors found that varying practices in pulpit and altar fellowship among Lutherans, "especially in differing methods of theological thought," were also obstacles preventing the desired goal of full unity.

Closer and more fruitful Lutheran relationships have had a prominent and cherished place on the programs at each annual meeting of the NLEA. Counseling and studying together, the editors have continued to seek the means of bringing Lutheran synods into a working relationship with each other.

In an effort to remove barriers to Lutheran unity, the editors in 1918, "recognizing the need on the part of the Lutheran Church of America of presenting a united front and of taking concerted action at least in externals," agreed to invite the presidents of the various Lutheran synods to a special meeting that same year "to take steps and devise ways and means for bringing about such concerted action."

Citing problems for which solutions could be found only through inter-synodical co-operation, the editors listed the following: "the need to emphasize the American character of the Lutheran Church in the U. S.," the desirability of a unified welfare program for American soldiers and sailors, and benefits to be obtained by the central compilation of complete Lutheran statistical information.

This far-sighted and courageous step actually "fathered" the formation in Chicago, on September 6, 1918, of the National Lutheran Council—an agency which today serves the common interests of eight general Lutheran bodies: American Evangelical

Lutheran Church, American Lutheran Church, Augustana Lutheran Church, Evangelical Lutheran Church, Lutheran Free Church, Suomi Synod, United Evangelical Lutheran Church, and the United Lutheran Church in America—with a combined baptized membership (in 1956) of nearly 5,000,000.

Acting on the editors' suggestion, the National Lutheran Council was made a kind of successor to, and expansion of, the National Lutheran Commission for Soldiers' and Sailors' Welfare.

The impact of World War I, creating a particular suspicion by the general public that Lutherans were a "foreign" church in the U. S. (particularly those groups of German background), as well as a need for Lutherans to provide a specialized spiritual ministry for their men in uniform, was one of the factors that motivated the editors to urge the move for closer Lutheran cooperation.

At convention after convention, the Lutheran editors continued to study various aspects of Lutheran unity. In 1921, for example, they reviewed the failure of the efforts of other Protestant groups to unite more fully—Methodist Episcopal, United Brethren and Congregational Churches, the Protestant Episcopal Church, the Presbyterians, and the Federal Council of Churches.

Searching to discover elements of actual Lutheran doctrinal unity, the editors in 1925 agreed that the Lutheran Church is "more united in essentials than any other church." This, the editors said, "is due to the fact that the Word of God is made the guide in all matters of doctrine and practice, whereas other Protestant churches largely take Christian consciousness and experience as their guide."

The editors recognized that such essential unity in doctrinal position among Lutherans is derived solely from common adherence to the historic Lutheran confessions. They agreed, in 1933, to promote unity through editorial co-operation, and by publishing news of co-operative Lutheran activity and events in other Lutheran bodies.

In this way, the editors planned to set forth (1) the present state of the Lutheran Church in America, (2) hindrances toward closer co-operation, "described in a spirit of love, not of facetiousness," and (3) positive steps to be taken toward greater co-operation.

The desirability of such closer co-operation was emphasized by the Rev. Dr. Ralph H. Long, executive director of the National Lutheran Council, who addressed the NLEA's 1933 meeting in Chicago, when he stated that the Lutheran Church of America, with its various national origins, "never has had unity, and this unity must be created."

Dr. Long suggested that the editors exercise the prerogatives of the free press. "If it is a real conviction on your part that closer co-operation is God-pleasing," he challenged, "become agitation centers for this movement through a sane, sensible presentation of the problem as it relates itself to the life and polity of the Church."

Dr. Long also observed, "Our people must be enlightened and informed on this subject, if the movement is to be intelligently fostered."

Recognizing that external unity of action in such areas as Lutheran welfare work and common representation before the government was a type of co-operation out of which more genuine unity might later develop, the editors in 1935 sought practical measures in which Lutherans might co-operate to further this goal.

Discussing the need for "a national Lutheran periodical," and for national convocations to be attended by Lutheran pastors of all synods, the editors enthusiastically endorsed a recommendation to the National Lutheran Council to conduct "All-Lutheran Seminars" for such purposes.

In 1941, the NLEA studied contributions to Lutheran unity by the American Lutheran Conference, the United Lutheran Church in America, and the Lutheran Church-Missouri Synod, sympathetically noting current efforts toward that end, and urged "All Lutheran groups to use every opportunity" to speedily realize "the day of better understanding and closer relations among the Lutherans of America."

The organization commissioned the Rev. Dr. E. E. Ryden of Rock Island, Ill., editor of the *Lutheran Companion,* currently president of the NLEA as well as president of the American Lutheran Conference, to attend the 1942 meeting of the National Lutheran Council in Pittsburgh, Pa., and to urge a study of "the feasibility of setting up an All-Lutheran Federation" in the United States, using the NLC as its working agency.

In carrying out this mandate, Dr. Ryden suggested to the NLC at the Pittsburgh meeting that such a federation might well become the American section of the Lutheran World Convention.

"We are firmly convinced," he told the Councillors, "that the present crisis in world affairs presents a definite challenge to the

Lutheran Church in America to close its ranks and to meet the problems now confronting it with a united front."

Further, Dr. Ryden stated, "We are persuaded that nothing will serve to provide greater inspiration to the rank and file of our Church in their response to the appeal (Lutheran World Action) which is shortly to be made on behalf of orphaned missions and spiritual ministry to servicemen than the realization that, at long last, definite steps are under way to bring about unity among the Lutheran forces of our land."

Out of this suggestion to the National Lutheran Council emerged the incorporation of the NLC and its eventual designation as the United States Committee for the Lutheran World Federation. The Council's actions in setting up its important Commission on Younger Churches and Orphaned Missions (CYCOM), the Lutheran Service Commission (in co-operation with the Lutheran Church-Missouri Synod), and the Bureau of Service to Military Personnel, are also due in some measure to the initial urging of the NLEA.

In 1943, the editors urged the use of joint prayer as a means of effecting "closer Christian fellowship and more effective co-operative action in the discharge of our common responsibilities and the utilization of our common opportunities as Lutherans." This resolution was sent to all synodical presidents, as follows:

"The Lutheran editors, in convention assembled, are convinced that one of the steps, fully authorized and enjoined by Scripture, that should be taken immediately to foster closer relationships among the Lutherans of America is for each Lutheran church body to urge its constituency, both clerical and lay, to use every opportunity to engage, in union with fellow Lutherans of all synods, in *joint prayer* to the God of the Church and the Center and Source of all Christian unity, to guide, strengthen, and enable us to effect closer Christian fellowship and more effective co-operative action in the discharge of our common responsibilities and the utilization of our common opportunities as Lutherans."

At the same time, Dr. Ryden was instructed to convey to the National Lutheran Council the sentiment of the NLEA "that *all* Lutheran bodies ought to be invited to share in any future Lutheran unity movements, such as free conferences."

In 1948, the editors voiced their conviction that "the times call more urgently than ever for the unity of the Lutheran church bodies in America." Citing "a world filled with confusion and despair, with the fear of war gripping men's minds everywhere, and with secular movements and human governments challenging the place and authority of the Church and seeking to restrict its activities and influence," the editors urged:

(1)   The strengthening and widening of the National Lutheran Council, "so that it becomes the powerful service arm of all the Lutheran churches in America."

(2)   The holding of free, fraternal conferences to further, by frank and open discussion, the union of all Lutheran churches in America. (The editors indicated the object of such conferences as being "to determine, in the light of the Word of God, whether the things that now separate us are actually divisive of church fellowship, and what steps are necessary to bring about a complete understanding.")

(3)   "Prompt and aggressive development" of existing co-operation of Lutherans on parish and wider levels. (The editors commended the formation of city, regional and state councils of Lutherans as "helpful toward this end.")

"We are convinced," they added, "that it is part of the inescapable stewardship of the whole Lutheran Church in America to face this problem of Lutheran unity without delay and without excuse."

It is safe to assume that the impetus of this energetic encouragement by the National Lutheran Editorial Association has had much influence upon merger and union discussions, out of which "The American Lutheran Church" is slated to emerge in 1960, as the result of the planned union of the American Lutheran Church, Evangelical Lutheran Church, and United Evangelical Lutheran Church.

Current merger negotiations between the American Ev. Lutheran Church, the Augustana Lutheran Church, the Suomi Synod and the United Lutheran Church in America may also be regarded as one of the fruits of this constant agitation for Lutheran unity on the part of our church press.

In 1955, the editors noted three aspects of change within the Lutheran Church in America during the past decade. These were defined by the Rev. Dr. Oswald C. J. Hoffmann of New York, public relations director for the Lutheran Church-Missouri Synod, as he addressed the 43rd annual convention of the NLEA in Philadelphia:

(1)   Differences between Lutherans are no longer emphasized.

(2)   There is a movement toward greater centralization.

(3)   The Lutheran Church is exerting increasing influence upon the world, and vice-versa.

The Rev. Dr. Edward W. Schramm of Columbus, O., editor of the *Lutheran Standard*, 1955-57 president of the NLEA, summed up the influence of the group in an editorial (*Lutheran Standard*, November 12, 1955):

"Our Lutheran Editors' and Managers' Association—now in its forty-third year—has proved in *practice* the blessedness and the practicability of closer Lutheran relationships. The annual conventions of this group are, in a real sense, a demonstration in microcosm of what a unified Lutheran Church in America would be. And the demonstration in microcosm makes one yearn for the consummation in macrocosm."

CHAPTER THREE

Self-Analysis and Improvement

SELF-IMPROVEMENT THROUGH continued evaluation of the church paper and its work has been a consistent aim of the National Lutheran Editors' Association.

Purposes of a Lutheran church paper were listed as early as 1915 by Editor G. W. Sandt. Chief elements to be included for best effect were: (1) love for the truth, (2) consciousness of a distinct purpose, (3) personality, (4) definiteness, and (5) faith in its mission.

Similar discussion in 1925 brought out the following points: That the church paper should be (1) religious, (2) Lutheran, and (3) journalistic, with the general aim of making a well-informed and faithful church membership.

Wider use of news-gathering and reporting was urged in 1926 by Editor Rasmus Malmin, who also pointed out the importance of making the church paper attractive and inviting, through the use of good paper and typography, striking heads and illustrations.

Editor Malmin also suggested presentation of doctrine to readers by "clothing teachings in the language of the day," and

15

by "driving truth home" in an interesting, lively and pointed manner.

The policy of the church paper must be one which puts the journal at the service of every activity of the Church to which it can render assistance. This was the advice of Editor N. R. Melhorn at the NLEA's 1927 convention in Chicago. This meeting of the group also heard a plea by Dr. Emmanuel Poppen, president of the American Lutheran Church, in which he advocated the teaching of religious journalism at Lutheran colleges and seminaries.

The value of publicity, coupled with the need for highly-trained writers in a day of keen competition from other agencies vying for press attention were cited by Dr. Poppen as valid reasons for establishing proper religious journalism training courses in Lutheran schools.

Specially-trained religious writers could overcome a common criticism of church papers, it was felt, in that many actually are "written from the preacher's point of view, and for the preacher's special consideration." As early as 1918, it was emphasized that the editor's job is to prepare his paper so that the common man can understand it.

Editorial policy was considered at some length during the NLEA's 1924 meeting in Philadelphia. Editor E. W. Sandt pointed out that the editor of an official church paper is not always at liberty to speak his own mind, but must speak for the body he represents—though at the same time, he should not be "muzzled."

The editor must give to the paper his own character and personality, Dr. Sandt maintained, pointing out that the editor's primary purpose should be to build up the religious life and thought of his readers, and only secondarily to serve special lines of thinking among the ministry.

In 1938, the church paper was described as an evangelist, whose main functions were to bring both Law and Gospel to its readers, to help the unconverted to come to a recognition of their sinfulness, and deepen the spiritual lives of those who believe. It was also pointed out that the church paper must indicate the connection between doctrine and life, and act as a warm spokesman for all the varied activities of the Church.

In a review of the practical accomplishments of the NLEA during its first 25 years, the 1938 meeting heard Dr. A. H. Dornbirer make these six points:

1.   Membership in the NLEA has aided editors in improving their work—more popular, concrete editorials; better makeup and editing; more discrimination in selection of articles for publication, and a more discreet handling of differences of doctrine and practice.

2.   Church papers serve the promotion of Kingdom work by their stressing of doctrine.

3.   Church papers have become more informative; more news is exchanged between editors, and more news is sought from others sources in the U. S. and overseas.

4.   Editors are promoting friendly relations between Lutheran Church bodies, with the NLEA a pioneer in the search for full Lutheran unity, and directly responsible for the formation of the National Lutheran Council.

5.   Editors have declared the attitude of the Lutheran Church in relation to civic, social and industrial welfare.

6. Church paper campaigns have resulted in increased circulations.

At its 1942 convention in New York, the NLEA adopted four theses on "The Editor's Job in Ecclesiastical and Secular Authority." These were:

(1) Editors should speak with a united voice on ethical and religious principles implied in certain national and international problems.

(2) All Lutheran editors should pay special attention to those political actions and projects which will affect the life of the Protestant Churches in this country and abroad.

(3) Editors should appoint a clearing house for editorial opinion which would gather, summarize, duplicate and send to government leaders such Lutheran opinion.

(4) Editors should study public issues and present editorial comment or opinion on these issues in their papers.

With respect to editorial responsibility, the members agreed, in 1946, that an editor is legally responsible for everything published in his paper. He can be sued for libel on this basis, and the Church holds its editors responsible for blunders.

An editor of a church paper enjoys spiritual rewards for his services, primarily through the joy of being called into the full-time service of his Church.

Unique rewards of an editor were listed as: being spokesman for his Church, and having a larger audience than anyone else in doing so; possession of incentive for spiritual growth and development; assurance that his "labor is not in vain in the Lord"; opportunity to heighten interest in the Church's program, shaping policy in his Church, guiding the thinking of its members, and promotion of Lutheran unity.

Technical aspects of church papers received much consideration in successive annual meetings of the NLEA. The use of illustrations received attention as early as 1919, and analyses of how to achieve greater reader interest were presented frequently. In 1947, Editor A. P. Klausler suggested that church papers were usually characterized by over-long sentences, abstract phrases, and a lack of a sufficient number of story-telling illustrations.

Three years later, in Minneapolis, in 1950, the editors invited Professor Harold Wilson of the University of Minnesota's School of Journalism to evaluate the typography and makeup of the Lutheran papers in the NLEA.

This expert suggested the use of more pictures, more informal layout to "jar" the reader, uniform typefaces throughout the magazine, and the employment of dominant article openings. Layout has become more important, Prof. Wilson told the group, and typography more restrained.

News sources and news treatment were studied by the editors as early as 1924, when it was suggested that "sufficient allowance" be made to pay writers of major contributions to church papers.

Mr. Albert Anderson of Augsburg Publishing House, Minneapolis, evaluated news treatment in Lutheran church papers for the 1950 convention of the NLEA. He listed six problems faced by editors:

(1) The editor's job is difficult because he must interpret the Church to everyone, both inside and outside the Church.

(2)   An editor faces continual pressure from special "interest" groups.

(3)   He consistently faces a deadline, or "time" element.

(4)   There is frequent lack of understanding demonstrated by correspondents, as evidenced by poor quality material they submit for publication.

(5)   Copy is often inadequate for proper editorial consideration.

(6)   Church paper editors are usually pastors, consequently find the proper "news" point of view difficult to obtain.

Mr. Anderson then listed six strong points as displayed by editors of Lutheran Church papers:

(1)   They have an earnestness for promotion of the Kingdom of God.

(2)   They have a strong love for the Lutheran Church.

(3)   They have a sense of the ecumenical nature of the Church, demonstrating this by reporting news of other Lutheran and Protestant bodies.

(4)   They give attention to and attempt to promote the entire work of their church body.

(5)   They usually demonstrate an excellent unsentimental type of direct writing.

(6)   They possess excellent news judgment in most matters.

Finally, Mr. Anderson listed six weaknesses of church paper editors:

(1)   Their papers are "house organs."

(2)   They must use too much "promotional" copy.

(3)   They often are guilty of subjective coloring of news.

(4)   They use too much news about pastors.

(5)   They do not employ enough "hard" editing.

(6)   They do not define what really is "news."

The need for a more critical church press was cited at the NLEA's 1951 convention in Philadelphia. Editor E. W. Schramm insisted, for example, that church papers ought to present "a sober and well-meaning examination of the life and works of men."

At the same time, the Rev. Dr. Robert D. Hershey of Philadelphia, guest speaker, told the editors what he expected from his church paper. "The intelligent reader," Dr. Hershey said, "expects the proper balance of solid meat and condiment." Matters should be presented, he continued, so as to evoke interest and provoke thought; church papers should revoke prejudice and invoke reaction by action.

In achieving proper coverage of significant Lutheran news events, the need for a central news bureau to serve all Lutheran bodies was recognized as early as 1914. Formation of such an office was advocated at that date, but recognized as "impractical" for the time-being in 1916.

Establishment of the Lutheran Publicity Bureau in New York in 1917, in connection with the 400th anniversary of the Reformation, was commended by the NLEA at its 1918 meeting. This agency, which is operated by pastors of the Lutheran Church-Missouri Synod, still functions from New York, and is currently known as the "American Lutheran Publicity Bureau," though its services lie primarily in the publication of an independent monthly magazine, *The American Lutheran,* and a wide variety of promotional materials and tracts for local congregations.

The National Lutheran Council established a News Bureau in

1921, designed to provide news to editors of its participating bodies, but by the following year the NLEA labelled it as "unsatisfactory." Its coverage of the Lutheran World Convention at Eisenach, Germany, in 1923, was described as "poor," and the NLEA urged steps to improve the service.

By 1929, the NLC News Bureau had risen in stature to the point where costs for its services were prorated among the synodical journals represented in the NLEA. Included in NLEA special requests from the News Bureau at this time were: (1) stories and fillers, (2) articles on the Augsburg Confession, (3) biographical sketches of prominent U. S. Lutherans, and (4) a "library" of photographs and illustrations.

Two years later, in 1931, the News Bureau was asked to provide convention coverage for meetings of the various Lutheran general bodies, so that proper news stories could be placed in the hands of each synodical editor. The News Bureau has consistently carried out this request from that date, supplying well-written, objective reports of the proceedings of the various conventions, with coverage improving from year to year.

In general, the task of a church paper can be summed up in the following quotation from the late Gideon Seymour, former executive editor of the Minneapolis *Star* and *Tribune*. Speaking to the 1946 NLEA convention in Minneapolis, Mr. Seymour stated:

"The church press has a task of making plain to the people that the political philosophy of the United States derives directly from the teachings of Christ. Many American leaders lack a faith for a philosophy of life. The Church is obliged to convince these people that it has the faith to live by."

CHAPTER FOUR

foreign Language Papers

IN 1914, OF THE 30 member-publications of the NLEA, nearly two-thirds were foreign language publications, issued in German, Swedish, Norwegian, Danish, Icelandic, Finnish, Slavonian and Lithuanian. Seven years later, in 1921, the members agreed that the foreign language paper still had a large place to fill, "as long as the church numbers foreign language people among its membership."

The function of foreign language church papers in "preparing the ground" for English periodicals was pointed out in 1937 by the veteran editor, Dr. L. G. Abrahamson. Drawing on 30 years' experience as editor of *Augustana,* Swedish-language periodical of the Augustana Lutheran Church, Editor Abrahamson emphasized the influence of the foreign language papers in promoting "sound conservatism" and unification.

In 1946, Dr. A. T. Lundholm, who succeeded Dr. Abrahamson as editor of *Augustana,* told the editors that the foreign-language church press "was born of necessity."

Describing the pioneers who came to America "to cast their lot with a polyglot nation in a strange world," he added that these early Lutherans wanted to retain their mother tongue and teach it to their children. Editor Lundholm indicated that the foreign language church papers helped them to develop a strong church life, because it was a medium through which they could express their own faith and keep in contact with brethren in the faith, both in the new world and in their fatherlands across the sea.

Dr. Lundholm emphasized the religious and cultural value of such church papers, underlining their "tremendous contribution to the inner spiritual life of Lutheranism in America."

Tracing the decline in the number of foreign language church papers since the mid-1930's, the speaker reported, "Their combined circulation today (1946) may have reached the lowest point in their history." He said the use of foreign languages in Lutheran homes and churches had "almost disappeared," adding that fewer and fewer contributors were able to submit articles for publication in foreign-language church papers. As a result, he pointed out, editors were forced to translate material from English in order to fill their papers.

Dr. Lundholm indicated that foreign language papers will be needed for a number of years to come, primarily for Lutherans "whose heart language is not the language of the land." Such persons, he said, have their spiritual lives nourished by devotional material prepared in their mother tongue, the language in which they "commune with God."

Stressing the continued need for such foreign language church papers among "the forgotten members in the flock," he urged, "Let our foreign language papers be their pastors, the missionaries who seek them out and keep them in touch with their own Church and its work."

*   *   *

By 1948, because of the declining membership of the Editors' Section, due to the discontinuance of several foreign language church papers, the editors amended their constitution to make editors of non-official Lutheran publications eligible for membership. In 1955 it was voted to admit as members "all editors and full-time assistants of official Lutheran periodicals, journalists serving the Lutheran Church full-time, and editors of other church-connected Lutheran periodicals of national circulation." In 1956, the editors were still struggling with the problem of membership, and, after conferring with a committee from the Managers' Section, appointed a committee to draw up a list of all editors and other Lutheran journalists eligible for membership and to submit the list before the 1957 meeting.

CHAPTER FIVE

Problems and Opportunities

A NEED FOR the church paper to assist in reaching young people was emphasized by the editors at their Chicago convention in 1921. Citing the importance of developing reader interest with the inclusion of material designed to reach inside young people's life and experience, four points emerged from the discussion:

The church paper, to reach youth, should:

(1)   Seek to enlarge the field of youth's sphere of activity in the Church.

(2)   Help to demonstrate the Church's confidence in young people.

(3)   Not hesitate to appeal to the heroic element in youth.

(4)   If possible, set aside a special department of the church paper, designed for youthful readers.

The relationship of the editor and the administration of his Church was discussed in 1927. Dr. N. R. Melhorn compared hierarchial administration as practiced in the Roman Catholic and Eastern Orthodox Churches with the democratic principle of congregational government in Lutheranism.

27

Lutheran administrative authority, he said, is not derived merely from the consent of the governed, but also from the willing contributions of the governed. "No church paper can be independent of the Church in behalf of whose faith and work it has been established," Dr. Melhorn asserted.

Editors must clearly grasp their relationship to the Church under this polity, he continued, stressing that the policy of the church paper "must be one which puts the journal at the service of every activity of the Church to which it can render assistance." He added, "The church paper is of the administration, not over it." The NLEA agreed that the church periodical should not be subordinate to, but co-ordinate with, other departments of the administration of the church body which it serves.

Continuing their discussion of administrative authority, the editors, in 1931, considered the appropriateness of "president" or "bishop" as a title for the top executives of the respective American general Lutheran bodies.

Discussion brought out a general feeling that American Lutheranism was moving toward the use of "bishop," but that it would be ill-advised at that time for any synodical body to adopt a resolution for such a change. It was pointed out that formalism was gradually developing in U. S. Lutheranism.

Before the Reformation, the chief officers of the Church were known as bishops, it was brought out further. However, since that time, Germans in some cases have adopted the title "superintendent," while Scandinavian Lutherans have continued to employ "bishop" for their leaders.

"Low church" influence in America, it was felt, had had much to do with the fact that presiding officers of Lutheran bodies became known as "presidents," even though the Norwegian Lutheran Synod had earlier used the title "superintendent."

The term "bishop" actually was borrowed by the Church from its environment, and referred originally to executives in city governments, it was revealed. The editors agreed that no spiritual or religious reasons could be advanced to reintroduce the title "bishop" into American Lutheranism. In fact, it was pointed out that there might be a danger of "feeding a carnal pride" in adopting the title, and that its use actually might be "foreign" to American institutions and the American Church.

In 1936, the NLEA considered the use of church papers in promoting the financial appeals of the individual bodies. Discussion brought out uniform agreement that properly prepared articles on the subject provided the best means for accomplishing the purpose.

"Appeals for funds do not interest $2.00 subscribers," one member pointed out, but it was also suggested that institutional advertising in the church paper would be very effective in fundraising appeals.

The subject of daily devotions in Lutheran church papers was considered by the editors in 1939. Dr. N. R. Melhorn of *The Lutheran* revealed that when he had discontinued inclusion of devotional materials in his paper because of the increased use of pamphlets for that purpose in the ULCA, his readers objected, and the feature was re-introduced as one of the most popular elements of the paper. However, Dr. Melhorn held that a devotional book is the proper instrument for daily devotions, not a journal.

The decline of the rural Lutheran Church came up for consideration at the NLEA's 1944 meeting in New York City. It was agreed that the rural church is of the "utmost importance," and that the crux of the problem lay in adapting the program of the country church to its new economic and social environment, with the local rural pastor as the key to the situation.

The editors agreed that the Church should encourage qualified men to prepare themselves for the rural ministry, and to provide such men comprehensive specialized training for this ministry in both college and seminary.

It was suggested that the resources of the National Lutheran Council should be utilized in developing a program and techniques for the rural church, also calling upon the experience of constructive rural organizations and agencies in the secular field.

"The rural church has a mission problem which demands that it become community-conscious, rather than constituency-conscious," the editors said, adding that when this is done the rural church would become and remain the strongest influence in the community.

The NLEA agreed to assist in solving the problems of the rural church by publishing information and by outlining and urging specific measures to aid the rural church in the discharge of "its important ministry."

The urgency of developing this program received further impetus in 1948, when the NLEA heard Dr. A. D. Mattson reveal that, of some 57 million Americans in rural areas, including villages under 2,500 population, only 17 million people are church members. The speaker called attention to the fact that the Roman Catholic Church had embarked on a long-range program to win rural America, and that "It is imperative for the Lutheran

Church to take a greater and more intelligent interest" in work among the rural congregations.

In 1920, the editors studied the attitude of the Church to the labor question, and defined this as being "one which is sympathetic with all who labor and struggle, whether with brain or with brawn; which views the difficulties of laborers with comprehensive intelligence; which directs and guides with the spirit of helpfulness."

Two years later, in 1922, the NLEA considered the attitude of the Church toward present economic and political problems. Several comments by members seem significant:

L. G. Abrahamson: "It is the glory of the Lutheran Church that her pulpit has always stood for making men just, righteous and true citizens by the preaching of the Word of God, and not by law and statutes."

Rasmus Malmin: "This is an age of specialization. Everyone has his special work in which he is expected to become efficient. So the Church's work is to administer the Means of Grace, and if it specializes in this, it is doing all that can be expected."

A. G. Anderson: "Unions, by striking and refusing to let others work, are so far in the wrong. On the other hand, the employers' method of lockout is also wrong. There should be some other method of settling these questions. Opinions among the people and among readers of church papers are much divided, and hence whatever opinion an editor might express, he would give offense to some and might only do harm."

Also in 1922, the NLEA heard a report that the success of a national Lutheran campaign for relief work in postwar Europe was in large part due to the co-operation of editors of Lutheran church papers.

The religious education of children in public schools was an issue which confronted the 1923 NLEA convention. It was agreed that expansion of Lutheran parochial schools was, at that time, impractical, and that an alternate solution might be to organize classes for children during public school hours. A. G. Anderson stressed this point when he told the editors and managers: "It will show that religion is as important as other branches of education; that is, the children themselves will feel that." He added that Lutheran parents should recognize that they have the right to request release-time religious instruction for their children.

CHAPTER SIX

Extending the Influence of the Lutheran Church

DESPITE VIGOROUS INTER-LUTHERAN publicity efforts in connection with the 400th anniversary of the Reformation in 1917 and the advent of the "Lutheran Publicity Bureau" in Jersey City, N. J. (later moved to New York, where it is now known as the American Lutheran Publicity Bureau), composed largely of Missouri Synod journalists, the NLEA found itself facing the fact that Lutherans and Lutheran news received little notice in the public press.

It was felt that two main facts were responsible: (1) "A large proportion" of U. S. daily newspapers "are under Roman Catholic management"; and (2) "On account of the war, the Lutheran Church is temporarily under suspicion, if not in disfavor."

Confronted with this problem, the editors agreed that Lutheran publicity ought to take on "more of a scope of an international service," particularly at the end of World War I.

In 1919, the NLEA adopted a far-sighted series of propositions designed to present the Lutheran Church's concern for a united Christian ethical influence in civic, social and industrial affairs.

"Without seeking to make 'ex-cathedra' utterances for the Lutheran Church as a whole," the editors defined their propositions as "guiding principles," to indicate how the Lutheran Church might use its influence in these areas of life "without the surrender or impairment of its mission as a bearer of the Means of Grace or of its confessional integrity."

These principles were:

"(1)   The Church's distinctive mission is to function as God's chosen instrumentality in the world to preach, teach, testify, confess, defend, and promulgate the Truth as revealed in Jesus Christ, and to be fruitful in Christ-like works of love and mercy. The salvation of souls through reconciliation to God in Christ is primarily and preeminently the Church's great task.

"(2)   It follows, therefore, that the Lutheran Church must not be turned aside from this task by any sweeping ambitious movements of a reformatory, ethical or humanitarian character, however laudable they may be, if thereby her soul-saving ministrations are in any wise to be jeopardized or weakened. She cannot admit that the faithful use of the Means of Grace is powerless to change for the better conditions in the civil, social and industrial world. Nor can she permit the substitution of mere method and machinery—such as system, organization, alliances either with the State or with Churches—for the powerful, life-giving Word which alone is effective for the beating down of the strongholds of Satan in every sphere of life.

"(3)   True to this conception of her duty, the Lutheran Church has clung to her mission of preaching, teaching, defending and promulgating the Gospel; and thereby her work has taken on the form and character of pastoral and parochial activity almost exclusively; but while her influence through the preaching and teaching of the Gospel will always be more potent than any direct activity in the peripheral sphere of extra-ecclesiastical interests common to all Churches alike, she cannot escape the responsibility of helping to counteract the civic, social and industrial evils that perplex the minds of Christians and good citizens everywhere.

"(4) The war has had the effect of aggravating the situation in this wider sphere of common interest, and we are facing conditions which demand the creation of healthy Christian public sentiment, to achieve which the impact of a concerted movement of Christian and other devoted citizens seems to be necessary. No single church body can hope to be an effective molding power in the creation of such a nationwide sentiment. All must contribute to this end, but without forming alliances, either secular or ecclesiastical.

"(5) The Lutheran Church stands practically alone in having made clear the difference between the functions of the Church and those of the State, and it cannot move in this peripheral sphere of common interest with the same freedom with which the Roman Catholic Church or the Reformed bodies under Calvinistic or Zwinglian training can; but it should be the first to recognize the need of creating a common Christianized civic and social consciousness to bear upon nation-wide evils. Luther's dealings with national and social evils were such as to point the way; but his influence was that of a prophet rather than of a dictator or manipulator in men's political or business affairs. His pardonable mistake, made under stress of necessity, was when he called upon the princes to regulate the administrative affairs of the Church, and in spite of safeguards he sought to throw around it, the Church passed over into the hands of the State, the last thing Luther could have desired. With this dire lesson of history before its eyes, the Lutheran Church must not be blamed if it cannot enter into civic and social reform movements with the same freedom as other Churches can.

"(6) The Lutheran Church, however, can ill afford to isolate herself and thus fail to apply her teachings and principles for the betterment of civic, social and industrial conditions. This means that she must in some way define and determine the conditions upon which her influence in this peripheral sphere is to be exerted. It is clear (a) that she cannot as a Church go into any organized ecclesiastical or religious movement to correct evils in State or society. The more the Church functions as a civic or social factor, the less it will function as a bearer of Christ's redemption to men. (b) What is needed to correct these evils is not ecclesiastical alliances, but alliances made up of Christian citizens with the Church as an inspiring and prophetic force behind them. (c) The fault with past movements of an inter-denominational character has been the confusing of civic and religious functions and making them seem as one. (d) The Lutheran Church can enter into no religious or semi-religious alliance where its confessional voice must be silenced; nor can it enter as a Church into an alliance that has purely ethical and civic and social betterment in view.

"(7) If the Lutheran Church, therefore, is to exert its due influence in this peripheral sphere—as it should and must—it must in some way help to create an extra-ecclesiastical agency of citizens that can function independently of the Church and yet be more or less under the influence of the Church. The war has taught us in a way how to proceed. The Churches co-operated with the State through commissions. Why could not similar commissions be created by all the Christian Churches to co-operate with the State (for it is the State's business, and not the Church's) in the continuous warfare against civic, social and industrial evils that threaten to undermine the pillars upon which the welfare of the three divine institutions—the family, the Church and the State—rests? Through such commissions, agencies could be created to cope with these evils, and the Church would not become involved in semi-secular or political movements.

"(8) The National Lutheran Editors' Association, with some such end in view, would respectfully request and urge the National Lutheran Council to make an earnest study of the whole question, with a view to defining the Church's proper attitude and policy, and to see what may be done to solve as speedily as possible a vexed problem that clamors for immediate attention. Otherwise, the choice will lie between unionism on the one hand, or a much misunderstood isolation on the other. The Lutheran Church can no longer afford to drift in matters of such momentous importance."

The national emergency situation in 1933, with its accompanying distress, concerned the editors at their meeting that year in Chicago. Reviewing the measures initiated by the Administration, the NLEA resolved its "hearty support" of the National Industrial Recovery Act (NIRA), urging upon its constituencies "likewise as Christian citizens to encourage our government, giving it their assistance in prayer, word and action, in the sincere hope that it will accomplish its aim."

In the same meeting, the editors called for "a well-formulated series of statements and definitions" to "present the truths of religion concerning sin, conscience, duty to God, to man, to the family, to leisure, to the State, and to fellowship." The NLEA's resolution cited "widespread negation of Christian ethics and moral obligations" in America which had "infected society to the extent that transgressions of divinely-established laws of moral and social conduct are not considered sinning, and that conscience is either stupefied by the poison of false teachings, or its dictates, even when based on religion, declared an invalid moral guide."

In 1952, Dr. Joseph Simonson of the National Lutheran Council addressed the NLEA's Omaha convention. He discussed Lutheran influence on economic, social and political issues in American life.

Dr. Simonson stated that U. S. Lutherans, who in the past had "generally let others do the leading" in matters pertaining to our economic, social and political life, are becoming "more and more vocal and influential."

He presented the following facts to illustrate the economic and social status of American Lutherans:

53% of U. S. Lutherans are in the lower income brackets.

43% are urban manual workers.

26% are farmers.

20% are trade union members.

56% have had less than 12 years of formal education.

The Church, Dr. Simonson said, while having to do with spiritual things primarily, is responsible for all of life. For one thing, he continued, "It must consider the influence of wealth: We must not trust in wealth, nor permit wealth to make one unfruitful, but consider it as given by God for service."

The speaker pointed out that while the Church does not take sides politically, it urges a responsible attitude on the part of all, and though Lutherans hold Church and State to be separate, Christianity and government are not separate.

"The Church should urge its people to seek public office in proportion as ability and opportunity warrant," Dr. Simonson declared, "and keep this responsibility before its youth."

The influence of Christians on government is of world-wide importance, he said, adding that the peace of nations "depends on the peace of individuals in their relation to God."

If Lutherans are to be influential in economic, social and political matters, Dr. Simonson emphasized, they must strive for maturity. He listed the requisites for such maturity as being: (1) knowledge, (2) responsibility, (3) being articulate in expression, (4) unselfishness, and (5) unity and wholeness, "seeing life in its totality."

Dr. Simonson noted five hopeful signs of maturity in present-day America:

(1)   Activity of commissions of inquiry into prevailing conditions.

(2)   Parental education on bringing up children to take their rightful places in life.

(3)   Growing recognition that politics is not a "game," and that the world crisis is serious.

(4) Voluntary associations, such as leagues of voters.

(5) Growing independence of voters, their emancipation from party slavery, though the two-party system is to be respected.

Signs of growing Lutheran influence in America were listed as follows:

(1) More Lutherans are now in public office than formerly.

(2) Lutherans are "listened to" in Congress.

(3) Lutherans are more influential than Methodists, less so than Roman Catholics or Jews.

(4) Today's Lutherans are objective, well-documented.

Dr. Simonson advised Lutherans to develop more positive activity, as was the case in the matter of refugee legislation.

CHAPTER SEVEN

Ecumenicity and Romanism

A NEED FOR Lutheran bodies to recognize their ecumenical nature was presented to the NLEA's 1924 meeting by Dr. John A. Morehouse, who became the first president of the Lutheran World Convention, forerunner of the Lutheran World Federation. He stressed that Lutherans ought to mobilize their forces in order more effectively to carry out the Savior's command to bring the Gospel to every creature.

Dr. Morehouse told the editors that they had a large role to play in developing a united Lutheran front, and he listed three "enemies" standing in the way of the church paper's task of demonstrating what the Church is doing and in bringing the power of God's Word to bear upon the public mind.

The speaker listed "unbelief, rationalism and worldly living" as the first main adversary, suggesting that "a religious paper in every home" would help to combat this enemy.

Dr. Morehouse cited as "the second great adversary" the Roman Catholic Church, which, in pursuit of its historic ambition of bringing all Christian forces under the power of the church-visible at Rome, was at that time "building up the monastic orders to emphasize the necessity of belonging to the one Church." He also revealed current Roman Catholic efforts to woo the Eastern Orthodox Churches and, "with some hesitation," to achieve "domination of America."

Over against this adversary, he called on Lutheran editors "to publish to the world the great evangelical doctrines of Christianity," adding in an anecdote that "Rome does not fear the Reformed Churches that go up in divisions and sects and finally dissolve by the way of rationalism, but she does fear the Lutheran Church with its Augsburg Confession."

As the third and final "enemy," Dr. Morehouse cited "Lutheran division, disorganization, and lack of vision for world problems."

*   *   *

The candidacy of Gov. Al Smith for the Presidency in 1928 brought the NLEA to consider the attitude of Lutherans toward the problem of a Roman Catholic seeking election to the highest office in the United States.

A committee of three, Drs. C. R. Tappert, N. R. Melhorn, and G. T. Lee, were named to draw up a statement for presentation to the press, listing the Lutheran point of view with respect to separation of Church and State.

In the statement, it was pointed out that in no previous election had the Lutheran Church attempted to exert pressure on political issues, stressing that Lutherans agree to the principle contained in the U. S. Constitution that "No religious test shall ever be required as a qualification to any office or public trust under the United States."

Indicating that current public agitation over the issue called for "enlightenment of our constituents in the present campaign, relative to the distinctive doctrines of the Roman Catholic Church concerning the seat of civil and spiritual power," the statement said in part:

"If the issue were purely political, the church papers could not be particularly concerned about it. If it were a matter only of the personal religion of the candidate, it would be contrary to the spirit of our Constitution to prejudice a man because of his church affiliation.

"The situation, however, is peculiar because of claims, teachings and principles of the Roman Catholic Church which are antagonistic to and irreconcilable with the fundamental principles set forth in the Constitution of our country concerning the separation of Church and State, such as: the opposition of this Church to the toleration by the State of any religion other than the Roman Catholic; its denial of the right of individual judgment, liberty of conscience and freedom of worship; the claim that the worldly government is in duty bound not only to assist, support and protect exclusively the Roman Catholic Church, but to suppress, if necessary by force, every other religion.

"Allowance may be made for the temporary suspension of the actual enforcement of such claims and principles, but they are recognized ideals, the realization of which must be the aim and constant endeavor of every faithful Catholic."

Further, the NLEA special statement said:

"The situation is further peculiar because of the allegiance a faithful Catholic owes, according to the teachings of his Church, toward a foreign sovereign who claims supremacy also in secular affairs, and who has world-wide political interests of his own which may severely clash with the best interests of our country.

"It becomes the duty of our Lutheran church papers to give their readers reliable information as to the attitude of the Roman Catholic Church towards the authority of worldly government, and especially the precious liberties guaranteed by our Constitution; to counteract misinformation, and to correct false and misleading innuendos, statements and impressions."

The NLEA statement concluded: "The church papers, however, will not and need not advise their readers how to vote, but must leave this to their own intelligent and conscientious judgment."

Copies of this statement were recommended for publication in all Lutheran church papers.

* * *

The issue of Roman Catholicism and its avowed purpose of winning America occupied portions of programs at NLEA meetings intermittently from 1941 to 1947. The Lutheran editors were urged, in 1944, by Dr. Z. M. Corbe, ULCA American Missions director, to "stop soft-pedaling on this issue," recommending that the church press "face the facts regarding the intentions and purposes of the Roman Church."

The following year, Dr. George V. Schick of the Missouri Synod's *Lutheran Witness,* told the editors that Lutheran papers might be well advised to "launch out in polemical articles" against groups like the Roman Catholic Church, "which are basically out of harmony with Lutheran religious convictions."

Even then, Dr. Schick advised judgment, "so as not to arouse in his readers the impression that attacks on the Roman Church are unjustified." There is a danger, he suggested, that an editor may "overdo his attacks, with the result that his readers grow weary of his everlastingly repeated and more or less similar criticisms."

*   *   *

In 1947, Dr. O. G. Malmin, *Lutheran Herald* editor, outlined a "counter-attack" against the challenge of "Romanism in America." He cited a "binding necessity" on the part of the Protestant press "to say what needs saying," also admitting "a deep reluctance to be an incendiary influence."

Dr. Malmin made a distinction between three aspects of the Roman Church's program:

(1) *The legitimate efforts of Rome to grow and gain converts.*

(2) *Its legitimate efforts to secure every possible advantage for itself.*

(3) *Its illegitimate efforts to gain undue power and preferment through wrong means and at the expense of others.*

The speaker stated that Rome's urge to grow is legitimate, particularly when it tries to win converts from among America's pagans. However, he condemned proselytizing of Protestants, rather than Roman conversion of the unchurched.

Touching on Roman Catholics seeking advantages, Dr. Malmin admitted Protestants also seek best possible locations for new churches, notice in the public press, programs on radio.

"If, because of harder work, greater skill, and more resources, the Roman Church is doing a better job of public relations—of making itself known to the public—than we are," he said, "it is easy to figure out what we should try to do about that."

The third phase of Roman Catholic operations were termed "definitely evil" by Dr. Malmin. As samples, he listed:

(1)   Rome's intolerance toward minority groups in strongly Roman Catholic countries and in strongly Roman sections of the United States.

(2)   Its persistent mixing in political affairs and efforts to dominate political life.

(3)   Its constant effort to get into the public treasury.

(4)   Its systematic effort to foist on America a culture and a morality "which we Protestants cannot accept, for the simple reason that we are Protestants."

Dr. Malmin advised "aggressive opposition" to all these phases of Roman Catholic objectives, and the strengthening of Lutherans in faith and knowledge, "so that they will stand fast in the faith and do not fall for the wiles of Rome."

CHAPTER EIGHT

War and International Problems

A DISCUSSION OF the rise of Nazism in Germany was held by the editors at the 1934 meeting in Minneapolis. The observation was made that Nazi authorities appeared to be fostering Christianity for reasons other than the primary objectives of Christianity itself.

Against this background—and attention was called to a report of definite signs of religious revival in Germany, Austria, England and the Scandinavian countries—Dr. J. A. Aasgard, president of the Norwegian Lutheran Church in America, was invited to discuss the situation of Lutheranism in Europe, he having recently attended a conference of bishops in Finland.

Dr. Aasgaard declared that Lutheranism in Europe was "standing at a crossroads." It was trying to determine whether to become a provincial group, confined to a certain country; or continue on the road to "a world religion and a world way of life in Christ."

He defined Lutheranism as "the whole evangelical philosophy of life, which our Reformed brethren do not know and under-

47

stand—that freedom wherewith Christ has set us free, and which is the genius of the Lutheran Church."

Dr. Aasgaard predicted that Lutherans in Scandinavia and America would have to shoulder the task of transmitting to future generations "the free spirit of Lutheranism," and he called on the editors to help bridge the gap between European and American Lutherans, so as to form "a compact Lutheran group, in order that, humanly speaking, Lutheranism shall continue in the generations to come."

*   *   *

In 1939, after lengthy and animated discussion concerning American neutrality in the face of the outbreak of war in Europe, the NLEA resolved itself "unalterably opposed to any legislation that may jeopardize true neutrality on the part of the United States, in order that our country may not be drawn into another European war."

*   *   *

The need for the church press to discuss international questions formed a main subject of consideration at the editors' 1951 convention in Philadelphia. It was pointed out by Dr. Herman E. Jorgensen that international problems affect the lives of individuals in many nations, and that Americans cannot escape the influence of world power politics which affect economic, social and religious conditions in the United States.

From this standpoint, information about Lutherans in other lands, as well as knowledge of other religious groups, was cited as an important ingredient to be included in Lutheran periodicals.

Deciding factor as to discussion of international issues should not merely be the editor's own point of view, it was stressed. Rather, the presence of moral principles and moral implications should be the guide as to whether or not the subject matter should be treated in the church press.

Two dangers were pointed out in this respect: (1) becoming involved in partisan views, and (2) undue caution by editors to avoid taking a stand.

Another speaker at the 1951 meeting was Dr. Stewart W. Herman of the Lutheran World Federation, who emphasized a need for the Lutheran Church to become both international and "itinerant." He stressed the need of fellowship with churches isolated behind the "Iron Curtain" and for aid to refugee and scattered Lutherans.

*   *   *

Dr. Theodore G. Tappert, professor of church history at Lutheran Theological Seminary, Philadelphia, told the editors at the same meeting that there is not much historical evidence of the influence of Lutheran periodicals on the attitudes and action of Lutherans in America. Generally, he said, the church papers have reflected the trends of thought within the Church rather than molding them.

He also contended that they had not been leaders in the fields of social action. In each of the American wars beginning with the Revolution, the Lutheran press had moved through four phases, he maintained. These were:

1. Before the war began, the periodicals failed to show any awareness that it was impending.

2. *As the war began, the periodicals cried loudly for peace.*

3. *As the war got under way, the periodicals supported the nation uncritically in waging it.*

4. *After the war, the periodicals have quickly dropped the subject, without learning any lessons from experience.*

To these strictures there were sharp reactions from the editors. In the case of World War II, one of them pointed out that he had openly accused the federal administration of trying to lead the nation into the conflict against its will, and that he had strongly criticized several successive steps of the government that eventually engulfed the United States in the war.

*   *   *

At the Omaha convention in 1952, the editors heard Mr. Harry Seaman of the State Department, who spoke on the relationship of Christian Churches to U. S. foreign policy.

"Christians are responsible for forming and expressing public opinion," Mr. Seaman said, which reaches the State Department through letters, newspapers, magazines and other sources.

The role of the Church is very important, he continued. "It has long since assumed the importance of the individual, but the world does not." He described the Church as "a special interest group for humanity."

"American foreign policy will not rise above the outlook of the Churches," Mr. Seaman declared. The Churches, for instance, can see to it that such matters as persecution of Protestants in Colombia and the fate of Arab refugees in the Holy Land are not neglected, he added. Church papers, too, he insisted, carry a heavy responsibility for informing Christians on foreign policy.

At the Rock Island convention in 1956, the editors gave serious study to the international situation, particularly with reference to the growing menace of Communism, as they listened to papers dealing with the political situation in Europe.

Dr. Hans Bolewski, director of the Department of Public Information of the Lutheran World Federation, speaking on "The Church in the Eastern Zone," stated that the preaching of Marxianism in East Germany gets nowhere, but that other considerations, such as preferment and advancement, seduce many people. Although the one remaining political link between East and West Germany was destroyed when President Adenauer abolished the Christian Democratic Union, there is still the strongest kind of unity between the two parts of Germany through the Evangelical Church (EKID).

The Rev. Wilfred Bockelman, associate editor of the *Lutheran Standard,* who had served as press relations chief for the 1956 *Kirchentag* at Frankfurt, told the editors that God is using this laymen's movement "in this particutar crisis in the life of the Church to stimulate loyalty to the cause of Christ." He, like the previously mentioned speaker, also pointed out that in the Kirchentag the people had found another spiritual tie that binds them together despite the division of their country.

MANAGERS' SECTION

CHAPTER ONE

Promotion of Common Projects

THE MANAGERS' SECTION of the National Lutheran Editors' Association was organized on June 24, 1914, at the Kaiserhof Hotel, Chicago, Ill., as a means of facilitating discussion and action on problems more specifically confronting managers of Lutheran synodical publishing houses.

From this early date, meetings of both editors and managers were held simultaneously. Among the charter members of the Managers' Section were:

A. G. Anderson, manager, Augustana Book Concern, Rock Island, Ill.

L. S. Dale, manager, Lutheran Publishing House, Decorah, Iowa

A. H. Dornbirer, manager, Lutheran Book Concern, Columbus, O.

F. G. Gotwald, manager, Lutheran Church Work, York, Pa.

W. H. Greever, manager, American Lutheran Survey, Columbia, S. C.

John W. Horine, manager, Lutheran Publication Board, Columbia, S. C.

Grant Hultberg, assistant manager, Augustana Book Concern, Rock Island, Ill.

Chr. Knudten, president, German Literary Board, Burlington, Ia.

Paulus List, manager, Wartburg Publishing House, Chicago, Ill.

Thomas Nilsson, president, Lutheran Publishing House, Decorah, Ia.

J. F. Siebert, superintendent, Chicago office, Lutheran Publication Society, Philadelphia, Pa.

Edmund Seuel, manager, Concordia Publishing House, St. Louis, Mo.

F. L. Sigmund, superintendent, Lutheran Publication Society, Philadelphia, Pa.

* * *

Elected president of the group at this organizing session was A. H. Dornbirer, who had also been present a year earlier at the founding meeting of the National Lutheran Editors' Association.

The need for establishing a uniform series of Sunday school lesson leaves and text-books was the first item presented for discussion among the managers. The initial result of this action was an agreement to use uniform illustrations for lesson leaves produced by the various Lutheran publishing houses.

It was also agreed that the ideal of uniformity in lesson materials and a common series of books and leaflets would be worth striving for, as a means of preparing more effective Lutheran Sunday school materials.

To further implement this uniformity in graded lessons for Lutheran Sunday schools, arrangements were made to have publishing house representatives present at a meeting later that year of the Joint Sunday School Committee of the United Lutheran Synod of the South, the General Council, and the General Synod, which met in Philadelphia.

The desirability of having a systematized list of all Lutheran publications which could be included in the catalogs of the various publishing houses was expressed. Through the efforts of a joint committee of the publishing houses, such a catalog was first published in 1924, under the title "American Lutheran Literature" catalog. Classifications included (1) theological and religious, (2) devotional, (3) historical, and (4) fiction.

Such a catalog was prepared each year, resulting in wider circulation of Lutheran literature among all synodical groups.

By 1940, it was suggested to prepare catalogs twice each year—Spring and Fall editions, and that each member publishing house should report to the others on all books and materials ready and in process of production, with details, so as to include all new titles in the catalog.

The following year, a committee composed of one representative from each of the co-operating houses was appointed to compile and print such semi-annual editions. It was suggested that all member houses should have uniform-sized catalogs, so that pages could be furnished to the joint catalog in electrotype form, thus saving time and money.

This plan was developed so as to include items manufactured by each publishing house by means of clippings sent in round-robin fashion. Approved items were made up into pages for catalog use, prepared as four-page electrotypes for insertion into catalogs of the participating publishers.

By 1948, a workable plan saw the publication of a "Joint Trade Listing," featuring materials produced by eight houses, with costs shared proportionate to the amount of space required. This catalog later became known as "Joint Lutheran Publications List," with some 2,000 titles, and it was circulated to over 17,000 outlets, including libraries, bookstores and seminaries.

It is of interest to note some financial figures which were reported at the 1914 meeting. Average gross sales of the ten Lutheran publication houses represented amounted to $120,000 annually, with average net profits reported as being $20,000. As a footnote to the report, the average manager's salary in 1914 was listed as $2,315 annually.

By the following year, further progress toward uniformity was achieved, and the managers planned joint publication of cradle roll supplies for Lutheran Sunday schools. Designs for these materials were approved in 1917, and they were first published in 1918 as the "Lutheran Cradle Roll Series." They were utilized by many Lutheran groups for a number of years.

Seeking a means to promote the circulation of official Lutheran church periodicals, the managers agreed in 1927 that the co-operation of local pastors was most desirable toward that end. It was pointed out that congregations with a high percentage of subscribers to the church paper often were among the best in providing financial support for the total program of the Church.

The suggestion was made that one week be set aside each year to be known as "Church Paper Week," at which time local pastors would speak on the importance of having the church paper in every home in the congregation. At the same time, a concentrated effort would be made to enlist new subscribers.

The Augustana Lutheran Church conducted such a campaign in 1928, on behalf of *The Lutheran Companion* and *Augustana,* its English and Swedish official organs. When the results were reported to the managers the following year, it was learned that the many new subscribers had been obtained for the papers, and that nearly two-thirds of former subscribers had renewed during the campaign.

Encouraged by this report, the managers voted to set aside the last week in October, 1929, as "Church Paper Week." This practice has continued annually since that time, and campaigns for subscribers normally are conducted during October by the various church bodies on behalf of their publications.

An important production item developed by the managers through common planning was Lutheran church highway markers. This project was first proposed in 1936, and it was formally adopted the following year, particularly "for the church bodies affiliated with the National Lutheran Council."

The Lutheran highway markers were first marketed by the publishing houses in 1940, designed as a shield-shaped sign, featuring the Luther seal and produced on heavy metal in three colors—red, blue and white. Location of the local congregation was imprinted on each sign, and these familiar markers have aided many Lutheran motorists to find their way to a Lutheran service on a Sunday morning.

Another significant achievement for which the Managers' Association takes some credit will be realized in 1958, when a

1,200-page *Service Book and Hymnal of the Lutheran Church in America* will come off the presses.

The need for such an inter-synodical hymnal was advanced in 1922 and 1923, when it was suggested that participating Lutheran groups could share the costs of compiling, composing and publishing such a common repository of the hymns of the Church.

The idea of a common American Lutheran hymnal seems to have gained ground in several groups during the next two decades. In 1934, the American Lutheran Conference discussed the desirability of a common form of worship, appointing a committee to study the matter. This committee reported ten years later that it favored both a joint Lutheran hymnal and liturgy. However, it was not agreed whether the effort should be limited to the American Lutheran Conference, or should include all Lutheran bodies.

The United Lutheran Church, in 1938, instructed its Common Service Book Committee to engage in studies with similar committees of other Lutheran bodies "for mutual assistance" and for "the publication of helpful information, but not for the issuance of authoritative documents." There is no evidence that the Committee carried out these instructions.

In 1944, however, the United Lutheran Church, meeting in Minneapolis, instructed its Common Service Book Committee "to seek the fullest possible co-operation with other Lutheran bodies, in the hope of producing as nearly as proves feasible a common Lutheran hymnal in America."

As a result of this decision, in June, 1945, representatives of the American Lutheran Church, Augustana Lutheran Church and the Evangelical Lutheran Church met with those of the United Lutheran Church, convening in Pittsburgh, Pa., to explore the possibility of preparing a Common Hymnal. Subsequent meetings followed, and eventually all of the eight participating bodies of the National Lutheran Council became participants in the project.

In 1946, at the suggestion of the Joint Commission on a Common Hymnal, a second group known as the Joint Commission on a Common Liturgy was appointed by the co-operating bodies to prepare a common liturgical service. Both groups have now completed their work, and the appearance of the *Service Book and Hymnal of the Lutheran Church in America* is expected in 1958.

When published, the new book of worship will become the common property of the eight bodies participating in the National Lutheran Council, and will be under the jurisdiction of a permanent Commission appointed by these bodies. Ecumenical in character, the hymnbook will contain sacred music from all ages and areas of the Christian Church—Greek and Latin springs of hymnody; German, Scandinavian and Finnish sources; and English and American hymns.

Production of the hymnal is a joint project of the managers of Lutheran publishing houses affiliated with the National Lutheran Editorial Association. As such, they have worked out such details as copyright, cost, distribution, and ownership of printing plates. A managers' committee for this purpose includes Dr. H. Torrey Walker (as chairman) of the United Lutheran Publication House, Philadelphia; Dr. Randolph E. Haugan of

Augsburg Publishing House, Minneapolis; and Mr. Birger Swenson of the Augustana Book Concern, Rock Island, Ill.

With the successful publication of the Revised Standard Version of the Bible by Thomas Nelson & Sons in 1946 (New Testament) and 1952 (Old Testament), the managers joined the Lutheran editors in a 1952 resolution "that serious consideration should be given to the desirability of adopting this version for the appointed lessons in the Service Book of the Lutheran Church now in preparation."

For many years, Lutheran leaders had championed the idea of having Luther's writings translated into English. The Muhlenberg Press published a six-volume English edition of his writings as early as 1915. Previously, the Concordia Publishing House had issued a 23-volume set of Luther's works in German.

Muhlenberg's six-volume English edition was severely delayed by the advent of World War I, editorial work having received a considerable set-back, and with the publication of these half-dozen books, no further efforts were made for nearly 25 years to put Luther's writings into the English language.

At their meeting in Philadelphia in 1955, the Lutheran managers and editors were elated over an announcement that publication of 55 volumes of *Luther's Works* was being launched as a joint project by the Muhlenberg Press and the Concordia Publishing House.

This undertaking was described as "the most comprehensive collection" of Luther's writings ever to be published in English. It was explained that 30 volumes would be issued by Concordia, and 24 by Muhlenberg, with Volume 55 a general index to the entire edition, and that the entire project would require about

15 years to complete. The initial volume was published in 1955, with the final unit expected in 1970.

Dr. Jaroslav Pelikan of the University of Chicago's divinity school, directing the translation for Concordia's portion of the edition, told the Lutheran managers and editors that the translations "are intended to speak good idiomatic, modern English, to strive to do to Luther what he thought should be done in a translation."

Dr. Helmut T. Lehman, Muhlenberg's book editor, in charge of Muhlenberg translations, pointed out that a large part of Luther's writings had been closed to thousands because of the language barrier. He added, "Luther's deep insight into sacred Scripture, his pen—probing into practically every significant aspect of human endeavor, is after more than 400 years being made available to the American public in modern English."

Another project conducted by the managers failed to meet with the success of the publication of Luther's writings. Need for a common Lutheran yearbook, or almanac, was stressed as early as 1914, to contain a register of pastors and congregations of all synods. By 1919, some exchanges of individual synodical yearbooks had taken place, but the managers continued to press for an all-Lutheran almanac.

Several such almanacs were published in the 1920's, but the publishers began suffering increasing losses following the business recession in 1929, with the result that all efforts to publish Lutheran almanacs were dropped in 1934.

A Directory of *Lutheran Church Bodies in the United States and Canada* was published in 1945 by the National Lutheran

Council, in co-operation with Augsburg Publishing House. This was hailed by the managers as a "fine piece of work." A revised version of the *Directory,* including a geographical listing of congregations and statistics of the various Lutheran bodies, was published by the NLC in 1953, with a further revised version appearing in 1954.

CHAPTER TWO

Co-operation Despite Competition

AT THEIR SECOND annual meeting in 1915, the managers
agreed that there was need of developing "more and better fiction by Lutheran authors," and appointed a committee to study
the problem and to make recommendations for soliciting and
publishing manuscripts.

Deciding to publish such works of fiction as a joint project,
the managers in 1917 considered the merit of 30 manuscripts
submitted. They judged only seven of these "worthy of submis-
sion," offering a quartet of the rejected manuscripts to Sunday
school paper editors. It was agreed that one piece of fiction
submitted, "Star-Eye," was worthy to be published. The book
was successful enough to be re-published in 1922.

The matter of developing Lutheran authors received infre-
quent attention in subsequent years, but in 1947 the managers
resolved to encourage "the granting of authorship awards by
any of our Lutheran publishing houses to draw forth Lutheran
authorship in our midst."

At present, the three largest Lutheran publication houses, Muhlenberg, Concordia and Augsburg, annually offer prizes to Lu-

theran authors submitting fictional Christian material for publication.

A basic discount system to be used in all Lutheran publication houses was agreed to by the managers in 1915. This provided a 20% discount on Bibles, with theological books to be sold at net. Clergymen were to be allowed a discount of up to 15%, with books offered to Lutheran theological seminaries to be sold at "jobbers' prices."

Pre-payment of transportation charges for books and supplies sold at discount to pastors and churches was recommended in 1917, but by 1929 the managers rescinded this practice by agreeing to charge for postage when a discount was allowed.

In 1933, the managers decided to prepay transportation charges for orders accompanied by cash, with such charges also to be allowed on charge sales of merchandise, if paid within 30 days.

Book discounts to publication houses in 1940 were set at 33-1/3% on books rating regular "trade" discounts, with non-Lutheran publishers allowed the same rate for up to five books, and 40% discount for orders of six or more books. By 1941, it was the common practice of all Lutheran publishing houses to allow 20% discount on Bibles and testaments, except for those listed in the catalog as "net."

This latter discount was to be allowed to churches and church organizations, pastors and seminary students, with the stipulation that postage should be charged when a discount is allowed. It was reported that trade discount on Lenski's "Commentary" was 15% for complete sets, if paid within 30 days, no discount being allowed for single-volume sales.

The matter of establishing a credit exchange service for Lutheran publishers was introduced in 1918, at which time the difficulty of filling orders from other houses for customers who had been denied credit was discussed. It was agreed that a list of "slow, doubtful and bad (no good) accounts" be made up by the various publication houses and submitted to the Association's secretary for circulation among all participating Lutheran publishers.

The following year, four houses reported the adoption of a "cash-in-advance" policy inaugurated to meet this difficulty, pointing out that the action was highly successful. They indicated that "under no circumstances" would they go back to the deferred-payment plan.

Uniform managerial account records were urged in 1928 by R. E. Haugan of Augsburg Publishing House, who suggested a reciprocal interchange of comparisons dealing with movements, methods and results which would be "of mutual benefit to each of the publishing houses." Advantage of this system would enable various publishers to compare their operating procedures, and it was agreed that such information should be furnished for the preparation of a correlated table to show the composite figures in percentages for houses participating.

The problem of securing the listing of Lutheran-published books in the listings of the National Library Association was advanced in 1916, with the project accomplished several years later. Attention was then turned to the placement of Lutheran books in public libraries. This could be done, it was explained, by providing "complimentary copies" to libraries where such placement was desired, following acceptance of such "denominational" books in the lists of the American Library Association. Other books, it was suggested, would be requested by the libraries if Lutherans would ask for them often enough.

The desirability of familiarizing Lutheran seminary students with the work of their respective publication houses, and of encouraging the use of periodicals, journals, lesson material and books published was discussed in 1937 by the managers.

To promote this policy, it was suggested to invite new students to visit their publication houses and to furnish them with free subscriptions to the official church paper and theological journal. Further, it was urged that church officials assist in making known to the students what printed materials are available, as used by the respective church bodies in which they would serve as pastors.

Technical problems with which the managers grappled were most troublesome during World War II. These included the matter of securing materials and making equipment repairs during the national emergency, even though religious publication houses were allowed priority rights in the latter situation.

In view of paper and zinc shortages, it was agreed by the managers in 1941 to publish uniform-sized catalogs, with pages to be furnished in electrotype, to save both time and money as well as to conserve materials. A steel shortage during the war forced the temporary discontinuance of the program of providing highway markers to Lutheran congregations.

Postal rate increases also created problems for the managers, particularly in 1926-27, and during World War II. In the earlier period, a proposed increase in second class postage rates was being considered by Congress, and it was decided that Lutheran publishers should write to their representatives in Congress, urging special consideration for church publications, particularly in the higher-rate parcel post zones. In 1942, the managers discussed increased book rates, raised from 1½¢ to 3¢ per pound, even though the second class rate remained unchanged.

On request of the Council on Books in Wartime, Inc., and the International Council of Religious Education, many Lutheran publishers provided German literature for distribution among German prisoners-of-war.

With the advent of audio-visual methods in parish education, the handling of equipment occupied the managers' attention in 1940. The publication houses expressed more interest in the sale of equipment, rather than the promotion of the material to be presented. It was pointed out that Lutheran publication houses would be in an advantageous position to suggest to pastors, congregations and other Lutheran buyers where equipment, suitable material and related addenda could be obtained.

The Lutheran managers voiced their unanimous opinion in 1944 that they were not interested in the production of films and slides, but only in the rental end of audio-visual materials, particularly in the selling of projectors and screens.

The problem of selling books and other materials to Canadians was discussed in 1945, and it was suggested that a Canadian Lutheran publishing house ought to be established, with the co-operation of American publishing houses, to represent all synodical groups working in Canada.

Further investigation revealed that Canadian groups, though intensely interested in the idea, were unable to provide funds to promote such a project. In 1947, the proposal was dropped, with the understanding that "the development of this activity must have its origin in Canada."

A survey of selling costs and salaries of Lutheran publishing houses in 1932, which marked the peak of the depression, revealed the following facts:

Lutheran Book Concern: circulation down 10%; shop salaries cut 10%; Board asking contribution of 10% on salaries in office; 44-hour week continued.

Augustana Book Concern: Salaries cut 10% on a 3-month basis; department heads cut 12½%; shop working 5-day week.

United Lutheran Publication House: Office employes worked one week without pay; shop on 5-day basis; June 15-Sept. 15.

Augsburg Publishing House: Salaries in office and time reduction in shop equivalent to 15% cut.

Employer-employe relations were discussed by the managers at their 1945 meeting in St. Louis. The training of servicemen was presented at the same time, with information as to the government's plan to co-operate with publishers to give opportunity for ex-servicemen to learn a trade.

In 1950, the Lutheran managers expressed hearty approval of becoming members of the Social Security program, which was presented in detail at their meeting that year in Minneapolis.

CHAPTER THREE

Eliminating Duplication of Effort

CIRCULATION OF BOOKS and other periodicals among the various Lutheran bodies by the respective publishing houses has been conducted in accordance with a "gentlemen's agreement," reached in 1926, that each publishing house should circularize only its own constituency.

Description and sale of Lutheran-published books outside the Lutheran communion was a problem occupying the managers for many years. It was made known that Reformed literature could be found "in almost every home" with "often a comparatively small percentage of Lutheran literature." It was agreed in 1927 first to attempt to acquaint the Lutheran constituency with materials produced by Lutheran publishing houses, before attempting to achieve broader circulation. It was also decided to work toward the goal of making American Lutheran literature better known among European Lutherans.

Joint publication of a book on Lutheran foreign missions, entitled, *Our Church Abroad,* was planned in 1925, with all firms represented in the association privileged to submit bids for the printing and binding of 5,000 copies. This project was designed to eliminate duplication of effort, as well as to bring together for the first time a complete record of foreign mission activity by all Lutheran bodies in the U. S.

The American Bible Society was singled out in 1926 as an "unfair" competitor in the sale of Bibles. In particular, ABS was cited for selling "de luxe" editions, and the managers expressed their opinion that the Society should carry only cheaper bindings of Bibles and New Testaments. The following year, it was reported that the Society might be willing to reimburse publishing houses for losses which they might have sustained in selling leather-bound Bibles at 10% discount.

The use of duplex offering envelopes was introduced for consideration in 1924, and the subject was discussed at intervals for many years, without any definite recommendation by the managers as a group.

In 1936, the managers agreed on uniform use of the "Cross and Crown" award system for Sunday school attendance. Direct dealing with the Balfour Company, manufacturers, was recommended for larger total gross sales, despite lower prices.

On recommendation of the National Lutheran Council, the managers agreed, in 1934, to co-operate in the rental of space at the Chicago Century of Progress World's Fair for the purpose of a display of Lutheran literature produced by all publication houses. Arrangements were also made to have salesmen present at the display to sell and take orders for books.

The following year, it was agreed to provide a display of Lutheran Sunday school lesson materials and periodicals at the World Sunday School Convention to be held at Oslo, Norway, in 1936. Birger Swenson became the representative on behalf of all Lutheran publishers, and was present at the Norway convention.

On his return, Mr. Swenson reported that the U. S. Lutheran exhibit had been the largest prepared by any church body, and also the most complete, and that some 3,200 visitors had inspected the display prepared by the U. S. Lutheran publishers.

He quoted a Mrs. Alexander Smellie, editor of English International Sunday school lessons: "I marvel at the way you Americans do things. Lesson material is well-arranged, easy to grasp, and the printing and binding is very attractive."

Mr. Swenson also quoted an Orthodox theological professor from the University of Sofia, Bulgaria, as having said of the Lutheran exhibit, "You've got the best *bibliotek!*" Swenson added that the professor "had spent practically all his time between sessions in the exhibit hall."

The managers agreed that though it would be difficult to determine what benefits each publishing house received through the sponsorship of exhibits of this kind, they were "justly proud" that their exhibit at the Oslo convention has "caused so much favorable comment."

CHAPTER FOUR

Looking Toward the Future

ALONG WITH THEIR editorial colleagues, the managers voiced concern from time to time over the future of the foreign language press in the United States. In 1918, at Chicago, they heard A. H. Dornbirer say, "As Christian citizens, we should be interested in the foreign language question, because we have a large element of foreigners in this country who will never be Americanized unless we teach them American ideals and American principles." He added, "We should also be interested in foreign languages for their cultural value."

Continuing, Dornbirer declared, "As publishers for a Christian denomination, we should be interested in foreign languages to reach a large class of people who cannot yet be reached in the English language."

He insisted that the Church should not seek to employ the use of foreign languages simply for the sake of perpetuating their use in the United States, pointing out that thousands of young people were being lost to the Church because of the Church's stubborn refusal to introduce and use the English language in its program of parish education.

The wisdom of these prophetic observations has increasingly become apparent, and the use of foreign languages by the Church had diminished to a minimum by 1955, when it had become the exception rather than the rule, and primarily employed to reach older church members, recent immigrants, and the like.

*   *   *

Mr. Dornbirer, first president of the managers' section of the NLEA, was honored by his colleagues in 1941 for 25 years' service to the group, and awarded a specially-prepared honorary membership certificate.

In reply, Mr. Dornbirer cited the "splendid fellowship" he had enjoyed through the Association, and revealed that his motto as a publication house manager had always been:

"Seek ye first his kingdom and his righteousness; and all these things will be added unto you."

He added, "The Lord has been good to me. He has blessed my work, and to Him I give the glory."

CHRONOLOGICAL LIST OF OFFICERS

Editors' Section

Year	Meeting Place	President	Secretary
1913	Chicago, Ill. (Maywood)	G. W. Sandt	W. H. Greever
1914	Chicago, Ill. (Maywood)	G. W. Sandt	J. W. Horine
1915	Chicago, Ill.	F. G. Gotwald	J. W. Horine
1916	Columbus, O.	F. G. Gotwald	W. L. Hunton
1917	Rock Island, Ill.	L. G. Abrahamson	W. L. Hunton
1918	Chicago, Ill.	L. G. Abrahamson	Emil H. Rausch
1919	Minneapolis, Minn.	J. Sheatsley	Emil H. Rausch
1920	Philadelphia, Pa.	J. Sheatsley	Emil H. Rausch
1921	Chicago, Ill.	G. T. Lee	Emil H. Rausch
1922	Columbus, O.	N. R. Melhorn	J. Sheatsley
1923	Minneapolis, Minn.	N. R. Melhorn	J. Sheatsley
1924	Philadelphia, Pa.	Emil H. Rausch	J. Sheatsley
1925	Moline, Ill.	Emil H. Rausch	J. Sheatsley
1926	Philadelphia, Pa.	Rasmus Malmin	Emmanuel Poppen
1927	Chicago, Ill.	Rasmus Malmin	Emmanuel Poppen
1928	Columbus, O.	Harold Jensen	Emmanuel Poppen
1929	Minneapolis, Minn.	Harold Jensen	Carl Kraft
1930	Blair, Nebr.	L. G. Abrahamson	Edward W. Schramm
1931	Rock Island, Ill.	L. G. Abrahamson	Edward W. Schramm
1932	Philadelphia, Pa.	G. T. Lee	Edward W. Schramm
1933	Chicago, Ill.	G. T. Lee	Edward W. Schramm
1934	Minneapolis, Minn.	N. R. Melhorn	Edward W. Schramm
1935	Rock Island, Ill.	N. R. Melhorn	Edward W. Schramm
1936	Omaha, Nebr.	Edward W. Schramm	L. A. Vigness
1937	Minneapolis, Minn.	Edward W. Schramm	L. A. Vigness
1938	Columbus, O.	Edward W. Schramm	Julius Bodensieck
1939	Hancock, Mich.	H. S. Casperson	O. G. Malmin
1940	Philadelphia, Pa.	H. S. Casperson	O. G. Malmin
1941	Minneapolis, Minn.	E. E. Ryden	O. G. Malmin
1942	Rock Island, Ill.	E. E. Ryden	O. G. Malmin
1943	Blair, Nebr.	N. R. Melhorn	O. G. Malmin

Year	Meeting Place	President	Secretary
1944	New York, N. Y.	N. R. Melhorn	G. Elson Ruff
1945	St. Louis, Mo.	O. G. Malmin	G. Elson Ruff
1946	Minneapolis, Minn.	O. G. Malmin	G. Elson Ruff
1947	Columbus, O.	E. E. Ryden	G. Elson Ruff
1948	Rock Island, Ill.	E. E. Ryden	W. G. Polack
1949	Hancock, Mich.	G. Elson Ruff	Herman E. Jorgensen
1950	Minneapolis, Minn.	G. Elson Ruff	John M. Jensen
1951	Philadelphia, Pa.	John M. Jensen	M. L. Steuer
1952	Blair, Nebr.	John M. Jensen	M. L. Steuer
1953	St. Louis, Mo.	E. E. Ryden	A. P. Stauderman
1954	Minneapolis, Minn.	E. E. Ryden	A. P. Stauderman
1955	Philadelphia, Pa.	Edward W. Schramm	A. P. Stauderman
1956	Rock Island, Ill.	Edward W. Schramm	A. P. Stauderman

CHRONOLOGICAL LIST OF OFFICERS

Managers' Section

Year	Meeting Place	President	Secretary
1914	Chicago, Ill.	A. H. Dornbirer	Grant Hultberg
1915	Chicago, Ill.	A. H. Dornbirer	Grant Hultberg
1916	Columbus, O.	F. L. Sigmund	Grant Hultberg
1917	Rock Island, Ill.	Edmund Seuel	Grant Hultberg
1918	Chicago, Ill.	Paulus List	Grant Hultberg
1919	Minneapolis, Minn.	Paulus List	Grant Hultberg
1920	Chicago, Ill.	Paulus List	Edmund Seuel
1921	Chicago, Ill.	A. G. Anderson	Edmund Seuel
1922	Columbus, O.	A. M. Sundheim	E. F. Bergren
1923	Minneapolis, Minn.	Grant Hultberg	E. F. Bergren
1924	Atlantic City, N. J.	Grant Hultberg	E. F. Bergren
1925	Rock Island, Ill.	Grant Hultberg	E. F. Bergren
1926	Philadelphia, Pa.	Grant Hultberg	Otto Leonardson
1927	Chicago, Ill.	A. H. Dornbirer	Otto Leonardson
1928	Columbus, O.	R. E. Haugan	J. G. Youngquist
1929	Minneapolis, Minn.	R. E. Haugan	J. G. Youngquist
1930	Blair, Nebr.	J. G. Youngquist	Wallace Larson
1931	Rock Island, Ill.	J. G. Youngquist	Wallace Larson
1932	Philadelphia, Pa.	Grant Hultberg	Birger Swenson
1933	Chicago, Ill.	K. P. Hundahl	Birger Swenson
1934	Minneapolis, Minn.	K. P. Hundahl	Birger Swenson
1935	Rock Island, Ill.	J. G. Youngquist	Birger Swenson
1936	Omaha, Nebr.	R. E. Haugan	Birger Swenson
1937	Minneapolis, Minn.	Alfred Adsem	Birger Swenson
1938	Columbus, O.	E. M. Laitala	Birger Swenson
1939	Hancock, Mich.	H. T. Walker	Birger Swenson
1940	Philadelphia, Pa.	R. E. Haugan	Birger Swenson
1941	Minneapolis, Minn.	J. G. Youngquist	Birger Swenson
1942	Rock Island, Ill.	P. A. Magnussen	Birger Swenson
1943	Chicago, Ill.	E. P. Hoeppner	Birger Swenson
1944	New York, N. Y.	O. A. Dorn	Birger Swenson
1945	St. Louis, Mo.	A. B. Batalden	Birger Swenson
1946	Minneapolis, Minn.	D. M. Shonting	P. A. Magnussen

Year	Meeting Place	President	Secretary
1947	Columbus, O.	Birger Swenson	P. A. Magnussen
1948	Rock Island, Ill.	R. O. Olson	P. A. Magnussen
1949	Hancock, Mich.	R. E. Haugan	P. A. Magnussen
1950	Minneapolis, Minn.	H. T. Walker	A. B. Batalden
1951	Philadelphia, Pa.	P. A. Magnussen	Albert Anderson
1952	Omaha, Nebr.	O. H. Dorn	Albert Anderson
1953	St. Louis, Mo.	A. B. Batalden	R. F. Stelloh
1954	Minneapolis, Minn.	H. T. Walker	R. F. Stelloh
1955	Philadelphia, Pa.	Birger Swenson	R. F. Stelloh
1956	Rock Island, Ill.	Albert Anderson	R. F. Stelloh

Birger Swenson has served continuously as treasurer since 1931.